ORAL
TRADITION

Other books by the author:

The Lipstick Papers
Flamingoes and Bears
The Gilda Stories
Forty-Three Septembers

ORAL TRADITION

Selected Poems
Old & New

Jewelle Gomez

Firebrand
Books

Earlier versions of some of these poems have appeared in the following books: *Flamingoes and Bears, Gaptooth Girlfriends, The Key to Everything, The Lipstick Papers, A Loving Testimony, More Serious Pleasure, Mosaique,* and *The Persistent Desire.*

Book design by Nightwood Design
Cover design by Debra Engstrom
Cover photo by Jewelle Gomez

Printed in the United States on acid-free paper by McNaughton & Gunn

10 9 8 7 6 5 4 3 2 I

Library of Congress Cataloging-in-Publication Data

Gomez, Jewelle, 1948–
   [Poems. Selections]
   Selected poems old & new / by Jewelle Gomez.
        p.   cm.
   ISBN I-56341-064-8 (cloth : alk. paper). —ISBN 1-56341-063-X
(paper : alk. paper)
   I. Title.
PS3557.0457A6 1995
811'.54—dc20   95-31481
                                                              CIP

Acknowledgments

Grateful acknowledgment goes to those who helped me speak out loud: Audre Lorde, Cheryl Clarke, Toi Derricotte, Alexis DeVeaux, E.M. Broner, Linda Nelson, Nancy K. Bereano. And to Diane.

CONTENTS

Gilda Sings: Escape 13

In New Mexico 16

Beneath the Williamsburg Bridge 19

The Woman Called Comfort 21

Rio Grande 23

On Lake Ontario 25

Riverside Park 27

Fairmount Morning 30

Gilda Sings: Longevity 33

The Servants 35

Hiroshima Red in Black and White 37

The Question 38

Tanya Rienzi: 1939–1976 42

The Loss of Meaning 44

Gilda Sings: Desire 47

Dream Book 49

Rooftop Sonata 50

Sonnet Blue 54

Getaway 55

At Night 57

A Parting 59

Approach 60

Oral Tradition 62

Gilda Sings: Dreaming Awake 65

Housework, a True Story 69

Absolutely Positive: The Movie 71

The Purple Testament 73

Flamingoes and Bears 77

Keystone 79

Gilda Sings: Escape

A PERFORMANCE PIECE IN FOUR SONGS

There's a dream I have of cotton, unlike what you'd know.
Balls, unskeined, unrefined, rough
and tender at the same time—but still white.
Dreamy puffs, perched elegantly in coarse leaves,
waiting to make me bleed.
It feels much like braiding my hair
but my flesh catches in the prickly fiber.
That I bleed is a surprise—such soft stuff.
Blood-spattered balls leave my load too light.
And you can't return to the rows, they move on their own
never waiting or helping. The rows breathe, independent.
You can't return to fill the sack
once you've passed by, once the blood is drawn.

The shape of my life is motion. Always
down one row, to the next. They called it forward,
onward, like Christian Soldiers, except I am not.
Just on and on, repetition, labor, yield.
Row after row.
Jump down, turn around, pick a bale of cotton.
Jump down, turn around, pick a bale a day.

Forward is only motion blessed by prevailing winds,
sucking tides, and vagaries of the body.
I left my momma's dead body but it follows me.
My good fortune: it doesn't fester and stink.
But it grows, blossoms out of those calluses
that pad my once-bloody fingers,
calluses that keep me from feeling.
My mother's not corrupt, only dead.
Eternal rest. The least she deserves
for her labor to bear me and the others,
her labor to keep white women alive
when nature told them to give up the ghost.
She had a healing hand. They pulled her in
to lay hands on their sickness and lacerations,
some self-inflicted.
The weight of wounds heavy
as cotton.

I am enamoured of motion. A rhythmic dance
draws the attention of the gods—Yemeya, Yellow Woman,
the many others who frequent sweat lodges
on Thursday nights, swirling in green garments.

Someone said to me once, "Gilda,
it must be hard in this world being black,
descended from slaves, 'buked and scorned,
benign neglect."
No, actually it's being two hundred years old
that pulls my patience. And I still don't know
all I want about the past.

There's a dream I have of past. Not a past you would know,
a place they don't want me to go.
But I can have my sisters in my mind
within the blink of an eye, or my mother's face,
dark Fulani, passing through Gulfport.
I can have language without wetting my tongue: sold away,
which is different from steal away to Jesus.
Rest, which is for them.
Sleep, which is for us. Dark—meaning to dream.

The past will not lie down and die. It follows,
easy as a wind circling the coast,
then sits up still against plumped pillows,
waiting for my embrace,
hoping I will lay it open with a skillful blade,
let the guts of memory splash onto me,
freeing blood for the stories of what really went before.
When I stole away, not to Jesus, I took the knife I needed
to do the cutting.

The past is a place I visit on my way to the next
one hundred years.

In New Mexico

On the road
it was usually the men—unshaven, searching,
licking the center stripe in worship
of the mythology of unencumbered mornings.
In songs
it is sorrow they leave behind—
sorrow like a girl's name
like my mother's,
Dolores, left alone, unable
to visit herself,
made less because she can't find the door,
read a map.

Then there is you and me
miscast but on the road.
I'm too embarrassed to say you remind me
of Sal Mineo and James Dean
backlit by the red/gold of desire held secret
between them—yet always in the open.
Asked to portray both mountain
and stream at once but not wear down.

Sunrise makes you tremble.
I feel it as you sleep beside me
on ground new to us.
See it in the muscle of your arm, tightening
as you press the accelerator.
The car leaps forward and
you moisten your lips as if to kiss.
I wonder which movie stars I remind you of.

We travel slowly west, then more quickly
as the blankness of the straightaway becomes
familiar. We lick the center stripe
eating up the mountains, storm clouds, gorges,
carrying anxious headlines from the east
we'd rather forget.

We sift through former lovers, fathers, bankbooks,
unwritten letters and the sorrow
that lines the highways
between Abiquiu, Los Alamos, Chaco,
trying to make each more solid, recognizable.

We sift gently
back and forth, turning in the light
as if we anticipate an archeological find
within the tiny circle we've drawn around ourselves
on our cumbersome maps—once spread,
not willing to close again upon themselves.

The Rio Bravo is grand and calm,
mindful of its tasks downstream, elegant
even as it moves around bank-bound quartz,
glass, outfitted anglers.

On the road
it is men who challenge us.
They meet the deep green of your eyes
with demands. They want you to declare
a neediness you are not feeling right now.
I look soft to them, black, not real.
They can't imagine me
here in this postcard—but you
remind them of the rocks,
the sorrow they've left behind,
some part of James Dean and Sal Mineo.
They need you to ask them directions
when it is they who want to ask:
How did you find the door, read the map?

Beneath the Williamsburg Bridge

On our second walk together
I'm wary but not of you.
Boys behind a chain-link fence—it's almost dusk
and they are so many in cleated shoes
full of cockish noises.

I'm grateful to be shorter, to fit easily under your arm.
The side of me not near you becomes armoured.
They poke at us with curious, weighing eyes.
All our parts fit, meshing gears—
left foot left right foot right.
You skip a beat to keep in step.

The J train above casts a waffling shadow.
Their lips move, but they draw no closer
to the fence. It is our good fortune
to look not quite harmless.

Across the East River the Domino Sugar sign,
a movie set piece, glints in the sun.
The Dead End Kids glare, not charming, not acting.

Your arm is tight around my waist, your hand
digs tensely into my pocket holding even my underwear,
our steps deliberate.
A ball hurtles through the air uncaught
as they swallow all they might know about us.

You are not a man
and I am not white.

The Woman Called Comfort

Legon, Ghana

My room is small with muted wood and a single bed.
Outside delicate lizards are birdlike
in their bobbing patterns up the wall.
The night air is thick with mosquitoes
and constant movement, comings and goings.
Ears open everywhere and traffic.
Only the road to Accra by *tro-tro* is smooth.

Upstairs her rhythmic sewing machine is a clock:
eight A.M. until eleven, one until four,
hand-sewing after seven with the students
who come to listen to her stories.

Her name was not smiled upon
where she found men too large a question.
Young girls in the afternoon
to learn stitches and womanly ways,
to fold the borders neatly, cutting
on the bias, emery balls and sharp edges.
Girls sniff the air, drawing needles higher,
an attentive bend to their bodies.
Sometimes the scent is clear:
men have been here, at some time,
but Comfort shrugs.

In her mind only the reach of cotton through cotton
as it creases the calloused skin of her fingertips
and Accra market on the weekend.
I go up some evenings
when the mothers stop to tell tales and
listen to the pulse of their own anxiety
dissipate under Comfort's passion
for their company.
I try to be inside their language.

Peswas clink in the purse which hangs loosely
at her hip, punctuating each movement
to pour a glass for someone.
Here they drink *apotagee* and chew the kola nut
away from clucking boy children.

She drinks Star beer, warm, from a tall glass
and keeps her shutters open.
The lizards rest lazily above her window
lulled by the sing-song music of her scandals.
On the road from town, in the bush,
the question of Comfort is too weighty.
In her room the Singer machine
is a chant of love. The women yearn
to crawl into her apron,
to rest against the brownness of her Ibo thighs.

Rio Grande

You are tall
even in the raft. Digging your heels in,
leaning into the river spray, as much mud
as water in the summer drought.
Back with each stroke,
your forearm ribbons brown
muscle under sweat.
The paddle sturdy, compliant in your hand
as I can be.

The sun beats down on your thighs.
Big, solid—turning with the heat to red,
long bicycle legs at home on the brave river.
Round calf leading to soft inner thigh
wet with the spray. Hard on the bottom.
Rocks rhythm down toward the Gulf.

You are tall
in the tent on the bank of the river
legs bent for me as we listen to the trout leaping.
I fall between your thighs damp
beside these mythic currents.

In dreams you kicked out against secrets,
fearful noises from the past—still waters
sunk deep inside you.
But now your wary eyes darken
with the scent of evening sage and humid desire.
Thighs big, sturdy,
compliant in my hands
as you can be.

On Lake Ontario

We are surprised there is a tide, deep movement
toward us low, without foam,
irresistible draw of cool water
at twilight.
My feet fit easily into the sand prints
of a large dog galloping full tilt
and I am hungry to run free on all fours
ahead of you into the newfound surf,
chase sticks, pose,
shaggy and dripping.
Instead we sit on a tree, fallen,
stripped of bark. Object
of unsuccessful bonfires
shiny with survival.
We straddle it thinking of sex,
feigning discretion for parents passing
with small children.
We manage always to touch—our elbows
or hips—and still eye the horizon.
The water reaches off
soft ripples to barges and tankers.
How can there be waves so far
from the sea.
We wonder.

You grip my arm. Woman fingers
pressing my flesh hard
so it bulges between like brown, kneaded dough.
You hold me to this place,
not rock but solid as sand can be.
When two mothers pass we lean closer together
pushing away their stares.
Incomprehension. How can we be bound
together here on this log
beside a tidal lake.
They wonder.

Riverside Park

1. Holy Saturday

Once, in winter, you suggested we walk
by the river when
the trees filled in
and the air was less gray. Now,
alone on a bench
with an old, white woman in an apron,
you are somewhere else.

She walks off, hands firm
on her marshmallow hips,
Not waiting here
as I do.

I am in awe
of the gray-faced pinhead pigeon
brushing close to me in his silent arc
cutting the air so smoothly,
of the twinned squirrels spiraling
down a tree—mirrored precision
and animal abandon.
They are never still,
scrambling past me
bound to the wooden slats.

When the wind blows east over the river
the chill, left in the air since February,
whistles through the budding tree limbs.
I watch North Jersey without you.

2. Brave Soldiers/Easter

The monument looks like the decoration
on a wedding cake
except here the shadows make grim
the ornate curls and chiseled figures
amid snaking branches.

A Puerto Rican man in leather jacket and cap
rises from uneasy recline beside me,
looks out at New Jersey and moves away, awkward.
I, too, rarely meet people I know here.
Late at night, one year, I caressed
the marble and granite
searching for the heroes whose deeds
drew these stones together in praise.
The river became the Charles.
I imagined I was not alone
and much closer to home.

This afternoon the old woman has a shopping cart
and lime green hat. She limps past
feeding pigeons, robins, squirrels,
watering the sprig she's planted
at the base of a tree.
I'd forgotten how often she's here, alone
with her park, strangers
who take photographs, with me.

I envy the children who fly full-speed
downhill on bikes together.
You are down the street or
somewhere across the river
as the squirrel snatches up a peanut shell
and streaks up the gnarled tree to the crook
of a limb that will hold it.

Fairmount Morning

The early sky is purple going to pink.
Outside our bathroom window
lights sprinkle down the hill
along Sanchez, far away, almost familiar.
The planes of the Bay Bridge are magnified,
I feel the wind rustling its cables.
Only months ago the light sound
of the morning paper landing on our doorstep
would wake me.

Now I'm up on my own, prowling,
examining, witnessing.
The cats are hidden away—their place
chosen anew each night.
They settle more easily.
I savor the carpet under my bare toes
and recognize the curve of our sofa,
the sharp angle of the dining table,
my first since my grandmother's house.

The air is so much livelier
when the city sleeps.
I'm relieved. You really are
upstairs in our bed.

Gilda Sings: Longevity

I wanted to be with her. More than I wanted sunshine,
more than the sanctity of church or kin.
But she was too much here. It was not my years but hers.
She was unable to come backward to the past with me.
For this I hated her. Hate her still, even though she lives
only in my memory.

I lifted myself up from anger,
from pies and doilies, from good, church works.
I lay open on a kitchen table slab,
begging to be looked upon, shaping that moment in my head.
But she spoke only of time. Especially the present,
its preciousness, as if I were a teenager
unlikely to comprehend tomorrow.

I own a wool cape, sewn late into the night.
She grew fond of seeing me wear it.
It is a dull, thick brown, but the clasp at the neck
is finely done. The buttons hand-covered,
even the cloth cut by me.
I have calluses on my fingers,
this time from the bite of the scissor
as I plowed through the bolts of wool
to shape the fall of soft material around my hip.

I cut for many hours, under a lamp too dim
even for my eyes, dark fabric drawing them to pain.
It was not for the present I cut this cloth
but for the night she'd finally notice the buttons
as she had them undone.
When wet the wool smells like the inside of my thighs,
puckering my own mouth in hunger.

I am not sacred. The folds of my flesh are eternal
but ordinary except when under a gaze—hers, my own.
Her youth is an arrow piercing my skin,
tearing through to the other side, exiting,
leaving me alone. Motion swept her along,
to some other place. I remained behind.
I envy her this leaving, this brief future she swallowed,
loving me, deserting me to meet some new day
I could not attend. I always expected I might catch up,
grow old enough to be with her.
Instead I am neither young nor old.
Mine eyes have seen a glory.

*We were never meant to survive.**
I do not die.
In her dewy face I see cotton bloodied.
I am a woman lying alone on a table with a cloak.

* Audre Lorde, "A Litany For Survival" in *The Black Unicorn* (W.W. Norton, 1978).

The Servants

for Emma Infante and for Emmanuel

The full moon has moved quickly through the sky
withdrawing its healing properties
into the west.
Clear blue dawn paints the high windows
I see from my bed.
Early air is cool and sweet in this the hour
you usually rose to cook for others.

The one time I hold you, I have to wait for them
to excuse themselves
and escape the closeness of your room—
the second bed lying empty, ominous.
The smell of medicine and flowers is thick
in my throat when I finally lean close
to your pillows.

Your young eyes are dark like coffee,
flat with anxiety. In the center is memory:
At Christmas we always drank too much
and whispered gossip to each other.
Rough outsiders, the help
made to sit stiffly at their table.

Now we're alone.
I pull you to me and press my lips
to your cheek three times.
I whisper my love,
too late now that you are dying
and it is safe.
Yes? you say as if it's a question.

I forget the restless visitors outside
and the thinness of your shoulders.
Your breasts, still full and round,
meet mine through the starched sheet.
My passion for you is finally shameless.

You slip a picture of your son
into my pocket as I kiss you like a lover,
but really a Judas who speaks of life
and cannot save you.

My hand is gentle on your breast.
Your eyes smile.
Instead of saying good-bye
I tell you again I love you.

The hard sun is up.
The air around me chafes with heat.
You no longer rise
for others.
The full moon has moved
too quickly through the sky.

Hiroshima Red in Black and White

on the occasion of a memorial exhibit of photographs of nuclear
devastation displayed in the Hunter College staff cafeteria

I admired the metal twisted like ribbon
around itself. Odd display for lunchtime crowds.
Quick-frozen images: an atom split
above an ancient/modern city,
pulverized chinaware, skeletal homes, eyes perplexed.
Marrow bubbling is not pictured.

I admired the miracle of the iris,
the scientific facts of loss
with geometric progression into our future.

Karen Silkwood's bones will glow beneath our soil
for years to come. Somewhere
on that red sun island
a child still burns.

The Question

for Gregory

Day after day, side by side for seven years
like a marriage, the better part of marriage.
We still remembered to look each other in the eye
over coffee.
In the first office we shared, architectural wedge
along a Dickensian corridor, why was your gaze
drawn to mine?
Because I'd just read a book of stories
from Latin America that made us both want to sing?
Or the way my flesh plumped inside a too-small jacket
vulnerable and wise?
For me it was the steadiness of your pale eyes
not openly afraid of me, curious.

I too was afraid and curious. That became a bond—
fear and curiosity. Embattled, overcome, succumbed to,
reignited each day and still we glanced
in comfort and surprise, knowing we were never meant
to see each other at all.

I've just been to one of those readings
where all the poems were written for the ghosts
of long-dead white men.
Words so sweetly wound
around an in-joke of prosperity
and white-skin privilege,
even I can barely resist their appeal.
What does it matter who
summers in the South of France,
vacations in Third World Countries,
or knows what the insides of words look like?

I smile the smile you've shown me—broad mouth
drawn into noncommital curve, marked by dimples
I do not have
and the pale blue of your eyes shining through.
I sit, you inside me, both of us listening
for a sign of life.

At a party where frightened people
take on the mantle of forgetfulness,
the only metaphor they have for life is sex
when there are so many: a berry pie, oozing purple,
damaging, enduring. A berry pie eaten by the dog you loved.
Just a berry pie that lives forever.

One afternoon you returned to our office
full of yourself, cheeks flushed, coy and male.
Lunch with an acquaintance
eager with a question.
Tentative, enthusiastic:
Will you father her child?

You said, "No, of course not!"
As if it were not an answer
rooted in much thought.
As if you were not proud. But I see in your eyes
you wanting to be the father of a child.
If you could.

Neither of us expected death. Foolish optimism
there in the indignation of your answer.
Not there in the dark with me
after you'd left the office
and night workers waited to turn out the lights.

I'm listening to the tape of "Sweeney Todd," your gift.
He baked food with the flesh of the dead.
Pies more pies!
A metaphor for life. Harsh chords and fearful passion,
madness organized into bureaucracy. Just like us.
Music written to force you from your seat.
Asked why a love might be so great,
you would say, "To create an opera, clearly."

There is a privileged innocence in the questions asked:
Why me? Why now?
As if the world were a perfect place.
As if those children starving in India
our mothers used as persuasion to our vegetables
were only a myth, as if they don't
have counterparts in West Virginia and the South Bronx.
As if there had been no Middle Passage, no Trail of Tears,
no Holocaust,
no railroad built on Chinese bones,
no California camps.

I want you to have a poem filled with the sweetness
of mundane tasks done with your lover,
of precisely sharpened pencils lined neatly on a desk.
You loved so many things: peace in the morning
when you wrote letters,
ideas to wrestle to the ground,
a man's hand firm at your back, the surprise of flowers,
a good Scotch, the music of Spanish spoken aloud
and questions.

Day after day
side by side
for seven years, the spirit number.
Like a marriage
the better part of marriage.
Todas son preguntas.
Abrazamos la curiosidad
y el miedo.

Tanya Rienzi: 1939–1976

Jenny died in a skinny Back Bay apartment
trying to say no to an irate lover man.
Her names were borrowed.
Her rent was paid.
Her dark green Cadillac
languished out front.
But she hadn't
hustled in years.

Jenny couldn't sing.
That wasn't why we went to hear her
at the hole in the wall
on the edge of the Combat Zone.
In the musty dark we could see
sweet North Carolina come alive
under a spotlight singing:

> *Blue moon*
> *You saw me standing alone*
> *Without a dream in my heart*
> *Without a love of my own...*

Her mocha face gleamed, a silver charm
nestled in satin smoke beneath tinny lights.
Her pouting lips stretched around
the ends of phrases, still believing

> *Yes, Jesus loves me 'cause*
> *the Bible tells me so.*

She was a star, bright in a paper sky,
a tiny country girl in her mother's high heels
leaping over the cracks.
On stage, above the hungry faces
and opaque, raincoat eyes,
it didn't show that she ate cornbread in a bowl
with collard greens, called someone daddy,
said her prayers, fed her son,
and sometimes sent me birthday cards.
On stage, under a glitter moon,
sequins were substance.
She said it was worth being paid in paste
to keep the tricks
on one side of the lights
and her trade on the other.
No one beat her with a coat hanger
if her voice got hoarse.

She was a rhinestone
dropped into a cheap setting.
Then she died in that
Back Bay apartment
screaming NO at her irate lover man
who wouldn't believe
she could live without him.

> Blue moon
> You saw me standing alone
> Without a dream in my heart
> Without a...*

* "Blue Moon" by Lorenz Hart and Richard Rodgers

The Loss of Meaning

lynching *n.* (we all know how to say it), death without a
    lawful trial, historically by hanging, but not anymore.

A horrifying murder commonly committed against black
    men in the U.S. See Emmett Till, Michael Stewart.
    And the eight other nameless bodies of black men
    discovered in the search for Goodman, Schwerner
    and Chaney.

And sometimes against women. See Viola Liuzzo. See
    Eleanor Bumpers.

And sometimes against others. See Vincent Chin.
    See Julio Rivera.

lynching *n.* a murder.

    Not to be confused with
    being challenged when caught
    doing something stupid.

Gilda Sings: Desire

Love is a mystery, the clouded peaks of mountains.
I had it for her, for others—
but desire is even more.
Savage. Self-interest. Elemental. Opening.
To take, to reveal enough to take.
Lay here beside me,
feel me steal across you when you sleep,
suck your breath as they claim cats can do.
Listen as I do this and be happy
I have finally come. It may be death
but it is also desire:
a fuel, not a place.
I push you back into the dirt,
the soil of your ancestors, slipping inside you
like a farmer reaching for new potatoes,
moist, solid prizes. Small scarlet reminders of survival.
Hold on to the rock at your head,
to the grass at your side but not to me.
I am motion, living
within the moments that have survived the past.
It's not difficult being black, being Negro,
being colored, being woman, being nigger.
It is difficult being and being and being.

Emptying out and refilling, reusable container.
Wanting.
It is difficult to miss the dour certainty of the rows
and not offer blood as a substitute.

Only this is assured:
desire lies in sweat, incoherent words
never repeated before friends,
and the loud song offered up.
On your back, heels digging into the silken dirt
you've forgotten you ever had a mother or mailed a letter.
You might have come from my past or your own.
The future may belong to us both.

When my mouth is open to let ideas out and you in,
that is desire—unstable gaseous explosive.
You give me your breath. I would take your blood
in mine whether it meant life or not.
Without our knowledge or consent desire remains,
a foundry, toiling hot, productive for only itself.
Metal clanging, plunging,
solid then liquid. Alchemy.
Unchained melody.
Desire is the only now I own.

Dream Book

for M.H.P.

To dream of a new hat means good luck
To dream of a hat too small is a disappointment
a hat too large means soon to blush
a top hat predicts good fortune in your profession
an elaborate hat means popularity
finding a hat foretells a sudden relief from worry

Finding your hat hanging in my closet foretells
calling in sick tomorrow.

Rooftop Sonata

for Mabel Hampton

"A woman who loves women is forever young." / Anne Sexton

I.
Mama she says from our pillow
echoing a cry I could never utter aloud.
Mama she says looking over her naked shoulder.
Light from the street shines
on the need in her eyes.
Mama she whispers before her tongue touches mine
opening the canal to a rush
that catches us both by surprise.
Mama she moans in pleasure.

2.
Ooh baby, baby.
The lyric oozes off tar pit rooftops
down the fire escape through resisting
city windowpanes.
Ooh baby, baby.
Love on a 45 and a sweaty dance.
Mama may have, Papa may have
but the baby that's got her own...
Ooh baby, baby.

3.
No, I don't know where she is.
Shit, she left!
That's all!
Bitch dropped me and left.
Just her name, that's all I got.
And what you want to know that for?
All I want to do
is get me some money to get me and my kid by.
Why you need my mama's name?
Shit, you is all alike.
My mama's name is my business.

4.
We usta do the two-step and I could shuffle,
buck and wing.
So we was always out in front of the line.
Light brown, dark brown sister act,
'cept I never met her mama.
We usta do the two-step to everything
and never touch no money but with our hands.
We usta do the two-step,
matter of fact, still do.

5.
I remember VJ day.
I pretended she was just my sister
and slipped my arm across her shoulder
as we looked out of the Harlem window
to the avenue below.
There was no light behind, only the glow inside.
We walked around it like young campers
at a too-hot bonfire.
She didn't pull away but settled
into the arc of my flesh.
VJ day below in firecrackers and broken beer bottles.
VJ day inside our hidden victory
behind crocheted curtains.

Women's handiwork always lasts.

6.
Ooh girl,
I heard that brown-skin woman
'cross the way, over there
is...you know!
Ain't my business, 'course.
But who woulda think that.
And she ain't no child, neither.
I seen that girl she call her niece.
Ain't fooled me.
'Course she don't bother nobody
and quiet as can be.
Wear those pants on the weekends, though.
Goin' dancin'!
Yeah, girl,
that brown-skin woman
'cross the way
is...you know!

Yes, I know.

Sonnet Blue

The blue-black mist of desire sits thickly
above a bed that is not ours.
Your back is turned as if only morning lies ahead.
I linger over you, unfocused, out of breath still,
afraid to touch the arc of damp skin.
Your knee is bent, running
from us in a dream that will last after waking.
Like a spoon I fit my legs to yours
slipping into the secret places that whet my hunger,
the new places you let me come.

In clear light, shadow is left behind.
We lay down in tangled valleys
but day moves west, inland, to make morning elsewhere.
I'd always hoped we'd wake together.

Getaway

for L.N.

It was either your pickup truck
or the way you asked me to dance that made me know
I would lie for you.
We packed the truck, headed north
where I could watch you ski, breasts bared,
full moon glinting on your freckled back.

Jukebox songs revolve in our heads
while I towel your body, then sit at your feet
lit by the flames.
When they burn low, we burn high.
Winter light washes your yellow hair
my brown fingers entwine.

You wake me from sleep to explain why
you prefer cross-country to downhill. It's cheaper
and the thrill more steady. Soft narrow
turns around low trees, fiery slice
against ice, playing the snow as you play me.

The gilded sun holds no promises.
Only your translucent skin and
corn-silk hair pillowed next to the
darkness of mine. Still, I would lie
for you and stay in hiding
till musky nightfall,
when mountains of snow
and moonshine free us.

At Night

I want to hold you
in a motel room
with the sunshine stripe
of venetian blinds
across your brown back.
Or I want the dream of that.

My large breasts press down,
you drink my sweat,
I push inside
hoping for endless night,
mining for release.

Against the white sheet
you are young supple limbs
and dark thought.
I fear your newness,
my need to make you old.
All my words are prelude
to this command of your body
locked in half secret by solid bands
of afternoon and evening
painted across the room.

Your hand is firm in the rope of my hair.
The highway circles outside
and day blinks by.

You bend over me
and the shadow is not cool.
I want to press my mouth
to your sighs
sucking in your insistent movement.

Or I want the dream of that.

A Parting

We sit across a table.
She demands I say
the things I always
have trouble saying.
How I feel about loving her.
About not loving her.
I can't open my mouth
except to eat the sandwich
I've ordered
just to have something to say.
I watch her hands move on the cup,
her slim fingers press the tea bag.
They are still the ones I feel on my skin.
Her eyes, filling with tears,
still have the searching light
that drew me inside.
The plaintive song of her voice
is the same: pulling me
pushing me.

I want to make promises
I won't keep.
Instead I am silent,
eating,
as she demands
I say how I feel.

Approach

Lying with you separate
I am made small by desire
standing full as a night storm
beside the bed.

Top-floor light
without reflective power
fills the room.
I cannot move,
you cannot be still.
We retreat to corners
examining each other
across the distance.
From where I lie
at my corner of the bed
straight lines are direct
and immutable.

The room is small,
close as your breath
on my ears.
The perspiration on your leg
where it meets mine
is a conductor.

Evening into morning pale and tentative,
movements now but no words.
Time has slipped away from us,
turned yellow with day.
We are damp with questions
neither dares to ask.

High noon, bright with no confrontation,
only heat. Long day
of unsent messages.
I will not move
'til moonrise.

Dusk makes me anxious on my perch.
You settle into routine
as if I'm not here.
The sun goes. The night light cool
and revealing. We try again.
I move across the room this time.
You open your eyes. I mine.
Our sounds come out soft
and round like the corners of the bed.

Oral Tradition

Shocking realization this year:
I do envy man his penis,
the freedom to stand
discreetly
and pee
against building walls.

Still, I would not trade
the sweet electricity
of my clit
as it sings with her tongue
merely for the chance
to deface public property.

Gilda Sings: Dreaming Awake

A road extends far into the future, far into the past.
One long and winding road. I move again,
this time in close circles
then twirling, dervishing circles, green skirts
swirling first around my ankles,
now raised above my knees
brushing your faces as I move. On point,
pivoting, burrowing into the earth with my toe,
my body a machine for digging.
When it stops I do not
but keep traveling, motion, traveling.
Salt over my shoulder, pale candles for our health.
I cut my hair from my head, bundle the locks
in neat packets and scatter them about the world.
I must keep dreaming to remember where they are.

My lips are parched and split
not from being black, being colored, being Negro
being nigger, being old, or loving women.
But from the lies I've had to tell.
From the bile I've swallowed.

As I watch this body, mine, swirl in remarkable skirts
I can see rows demarcated by the hidden locks of my hair.
There is that place they would not allow me to go.
There is the horizon I was too bitter to see.
In the east a sun still rises, I'm told.
And following it, a sweet low moon.

Why, in the dream, do I still carry a knife for gutting?
If I peer intently I see past myself
deep into eyes that belong to others on the road
who dream as I do: there's a dark woman, her breasts freed,
wearing a purple and pink polka-dot dress
a celebration of the flesh, ignoring the scorn
of her sisters and brothers, moving away
in her own direction, possibly turning on her toe.

A sweet-voiced guy driving a cab with three hundred people
all riding for free. And he's smiling.
He's eaten the bodies of their tormentors.

A very white-faced woman who still remembers being a girl.
That wisdom sits inside her, a guide.

There are many. Like me. Our knives remained sheathed.
Our eyes open.

I brush the fresh-cut hairs from my face with bloody fingers.
The startling red streaks mark me and the cotton—
a ritual painting.
Trails are made deep into the rows, where others
have passed. Do I ever laugh in the dream?
Maybe at the thoughtful baby biting her mother's breast
to prepare her for separation anxiety.
The procession of others,
the procession of myself—mirthful?
Perhaps.

There's a dream I have of who I am.
In it I'm a woman with my breasts bound tight
to my body—invincible. Armoured dreamer
with no obstacles in my path.
A woman with my breasts bound tight to my body,
who can breathe only with care, wasting no air,
making no easy motion.
I am not a woman ripe for splitting open
but a tightly wrapped package of everything we need to know.

When I stop twirling, the dream may end
or it may have a life of its own.
Black, red, purple songs that insist upon being sung
by lips, no matter how split.
The words may be as bitter as bile
or as sweet as my skin.

And through the song blood flows,
a cappella, unashamed, unafraid.
We may be despairing but blood is sanguine.

When I stop my remarkable green skirts
and dull brown cape nestle damply against my thighs.
I suck on the sweet bloodied tips of my fingers
for sustenance.
They are the earthy mushrooms of vision.

Our escape always lies ahead.

Housework, a True Story

She folded her panties and sweaters
neatly on the kitchen table
soon after he went out.
She folded her jacket,
her one silk scarf, some socks
and a blanket she'd always owned.
She folded her jeans and her blouses
then wrapped a towel around
a cardboard jewelry box
full of papier-mâché.
Her shoes, purse, her photo album
rested on formica.

She worked until she heard
the key in the door.
Their smells of smoke and Scotch
clouded the house
obscuring her anxious smile.
Their private laughter raced
through rooms
and bounced off plaster
making it hard to hear.

Later they weren't sure they'd seen
her leave in her winter coat,
although it was late spring.

She walked out with a green plastic bag
and over her shoulder
offered one explanation:
"I'm taking out the garbage."

Then was gone.

Absolutely Positive: The Movie

for Doris

on the occasion of the post-premiere party

A trim, red-haired woman, balancing a plate
of Swedish meatballs and a glass of red wine, asks:
Did I enjoy being in the film?

I was not in the film.

Am I sure? she asks, puzzled that there might be
two fat, black women at the same Upper West Side party.
I resist saying "absolutely positive,"
and rush back to you to share the update:
Nothing has changed.
We cut her to shreds between mouthfuls
of sliced turkey and crudité,
masked by wicked laughter.

You are chestnut dark, glistening skin
delivered from the river Niger, nervous gestures
and your straightened hair, a black patent leather frame
around your face.

I am not.

You are straight, wearing your best dress and worry lines.
Children—what will they be without you?
And your husband who just can't decide?
You are fighting with welfare about the papers
they keep misplacing, the requirements they keep shifting
and the payments they don't make.
Uncomfortable in the room full of well-meaning
white people who can't remember what you look like.
You're from Oakland and miss the gentle rhythm of the bay,
the hazy light that rolls in with the mist,
and the sure sound of loud music.

You are positive.
I am not.

We are comrades in our laughter
but I understand the gulf between us
and their lack of recognition.
It is some element in our smiles—
a welcome, a release, a seduction.
There is a curve in your mouth
mirrored in mine. Almost an opening.
A place where rage lives, baffled and bound.

The Purple Testament

I. Ghana, 1973

I remember the castle now only as a snapshot,
and the pounding of the ocean.
On Cape Coast, standing in fresh grass,
the shadow of mortar and rock, welcoming.
Not fearsome as I'd imagined.

It is the bricks, I come to notice, holding it all together.
Inside, the guide offers demonstrations.
He knows the lore, is titillated by the sale
and use of his women in a distant past.
His daily satisfaction: the somber white faces
grouped at his feet to hear what can barely be told.
Among them my darkness.
He looks away, recites facts—
how many sold, their chains on cold rock,
how many leapt to death from the walls of the fortress,
from the decks of ships.

Small Christmas bulbs circle a dank, sunken room.
When it is made black, we gasp.
I close my eyes and settle in the dark,
touch the wall to avoid vertigo.
Coolness first, then rough angles, damp.
I cling to them. The ancient rock, the grasping energy.

My fingertips meet the hard surface and beneath it skin,
wet with urine and blood. Schism. My flesh to their stone.
A part of me slips in with them to harden the mortar,
leaving the rest of me free, afraid of the sun
that returns when the bulbs are lit.
Left behind by those who've gone before.

2. Chaco Canyon, New Mexico, 1986

Tight lines of shale melded together inside the mounds
until uncovered. Their dust is silt, soil, rock
then brick slabbed and interwoven like lace.
More faces again reveal that lust
for fabled cultures, asleep in a remote past.
Through the awkward opening to the inner room where corn
was stored or garbage housed, we listen to the drone
of legends well-learned. When you sit by the wall
only I notice the flush, the crystals of sweat.
You gulp for air, rest your head
on the layers of rock that rise behind,
holding a past not meant to be displayed
without ceremony.

You lean back in time,
brown stones imprint the nappy dark
of your head. Your eyes close. I'm afraid
so help you up,
hold tight to still your trembling.
The air between the cracks moves where
you had slipped inside. We strain but barely hear the wind.
There is Anasazi life in these canyons still.
It pulls through the rocks
that look only like a wall.

3. Manhattan, 1986

On West End Avenue, cresting 98th Street,
the valley glitters. I'm outside
among the many faceless windows that
shook last year with a sudden quake.
Unforeseen encroachment on the tidy disarray. Reminder.

Red brick I've grown to love, instead of mud and shale,
teeters below me, gothic canyon with firelight
flickering on cement.
A river tossing in its bed, carving rock and asphalt
before it gives itself over. Traffic rhythms pulse,
propelling me inward. I peel back one level
to iron tracks, another to the swimming sewer.
Excavate, cut through to waste,
minerals and burial grounds—
Ibo, Fulani, the Six Nations.

It is a relief to know all rock is a door
living and growing around me as I cross the avenue.
Towering walls cast shadows on synthetic abutments.
Little to remember.
It is the rock that holds us.

Flamingoes and Bears

Flamingoes and bears
meet secretly
on odd street corners.
Horses and chickens
elephants and geese
look shocked and appalled.

Ostriches don't look at all.

Bear and flamingo
ignore greedy gazes
from disgruntled parents
and frightened sly weasels
who hiss
as the couple strolls by.

Chance brought them here
from forest and sea,
but science won't agree
where
bears and flamingoes
learned how simple
building a nest
in a den can be.

Now flamingo and bear
sleep forever entwined
in all sorts of climes
be it rainy or snowy or sunny,
happy to know
there's room in this world
for a bear who likes palm trees

and a bird who loves honey.

Keystone

for Diane

The first picture you take of me
in our new home I am sitting in front
of the huge, unworking fireplace. Laughing
at nothing in particular: the boxes
are finally unpacked, there's no more dust.
That we are finally together.
I'm not posed or self-conscious of the gap
in my teeth. I'm usually afraid
it makes me look loud, unladylike.
I seem to be in motion, shaking
with hilarity.
Behind me the impressive masonry
of the hearth. Handcrafted bricks, reddish brown
snuggled tight with creamy beige, some smooth
others textured as if still in the quarry.
They build, each upon the one before. Worn
to match, colors distinct but grown together.
They have such straight, mortared angles
yet they curve to frame an arc,
now shuttered until work can be done.
They feel fluid.
Suspended at their center—the keystone, not
classically shaped but muted double triangles
wedged one atop the other. Sharp points removed
to make the union easier.

Firebrand Books is an award-winning feminist and lesbian publishing house celebrating its tenth anniversary year in 1995. We are committed to producing quality work in a wide variety of genres by ethnically and racially diverse authors.

A free catalog is available on request from Firebrand Books, 141 The Commons, Ithaca, New York 14850, (607) 272-0000.